FREEDOM'S
PROMISE

# ARETHA FRANKLIN
## LEGENDARY SINGER

BY DUCHESS HARRIS, JD, PHD

WITH TAMMY GAGNE

**Core Library**

An Imprint of Abdo Publishing
abdobooks.com

Cover image: Aretha Franklin became well known in
the 1960s as a soul and pop singer.

abdobooks.com

Published by Abdo Publishing, a division of ABDO, PO Box 398166, Minneapolis, Minnesota 55439. Copyright © 2020 by Abdo Consulting Group, Inc. International copyrights reserved in all countries. No part of this book may be reproduced in any form without written permission from the publisher. Core Library™ is a trademark and logo of Abdo Publishing.

Printed in the United States of America, North Mankato, Minnesota
092019
012020

THIS BOOK CONTAINS
RECYCLED MATERIALS

Cover Photo: Ron Howard/Redferns/Getty Images
Interior Photos: Ron Howard/Redferns/Getty Images, 1; Dave Pickoff/AP Images, 5; Pat Benic/picture-alliance/dpa/AP Images, 6–7; Marcy Nighswander/AP Images, 10, 43; Olivier Douliery/Abacausa.com/Newscom, 12; Anthony Barboza/Archive Photos/Getty Images, 14–15; Red Line Editorial, 16, 39; Rebecca Cook/Reuters/Newscom, 18; Donaldson Collection/Michael Ochs Archives/Getty Images, 22–23; RBM Vintage Images/Alamy, 25; Michael Ochs Archives/Getty Images, 27, 32–33, 35; IFA Film/United Archives/Newscom, 37

Editor: Maddie Spalding
Series Designer: Ryan Gale

Library of Congress Control Number: 2019941997

Publisher's Cataloging-in-Publication Data

Names: Harris, Duchess, author. | Gagne, Tammy, author.
Title: Aretha Franklin: legendary singer/ by Duchess Harris and Tammy Gagne.
Other title: legendary singer
Description: Minneapolis, Minnesota : Abdo Publishing, 2020 | Series: Freedom's promise | Includes online resources and index.
Identifiers: ISBN 9781532190773 (lib. bdg.) | ISBN 9781532176623 (ebook)
Subjects: LCSH: Franklin, Aretha--Juvenile literature. | Soul musicians--United States--Biography--Juvenile literature. | Women singers--United States--Biography--Juvenile literature. | African American musicians--Biography--Juvenile literature. | Songwriters--Biography--Juvenile literature. | Civil rights activists--Biography--Juvenile literature.
Classification: DDC 782.421644 [B]--dc23

# CONTENTS

# A LETTER FROM DUCHESS

On August 31, 2018, hundreds of people gathered in Detroit, Michigan. They came to honor the life and legacy of singer Aretha Franklin. Franklin's funeral was more than six hours long. It was broadcast around the world. Many important public figures attended the ceremony. If you listen to their tributes, one thing becomes clear: Franklin was more than a singer. She was a legend.

Franklin was a talented singer with a powerful voice. But her musical abilities were only one part of what made her legendary. In her music, she shared messages of empowerment. Franklin's songs inspired civil rights and women's rights activists in the 1960s. Franklin also supported civil rights activists such as Martin Luther King Jr. In these ways, she influenced American political culture.

Franklin left us with a body of music that challenges us to commit to freedom's promise for all Americans. Please join me in exploring the life and influence of this extraordinary singer and activist.

*Duchess Harris*

Aretha Franklin holds a Grammy Award that she won for her cover of the song "Bridge Over Troubled Water" in 1972.

# A POWERFUL VOICE

On January 20, 2009, a crowd of people filled the National Mall in front of the US Capitol Building in Washington, DC. They had gathered to witness a historic event. It was Inauguration Day. Barack Obama was about to be sworn in as the forty-fourth president of the United States. He was the first African American to be elected president of the nation. When it came time to choose someone to sing at his inauguration ceremony, Obama did not need to think it over. He told his staff right away that he wanted Aretha Franklin, "the Queen of Soul."

**More than 1 million people watched Franklin sing at the inauguration of President Barack Obama.**

Franklin knew how important this day was. It showed just how far African Americans had come. Franklin had grown up during the height of the American civil rights movement in the 1950s and 1960s. The civil rights movement was a period of mass protest. Activists brought attention to the mistreatment of African Americans. African Americans faced widespread discrimination. They were often denied jobs and other opportunities because of their race. Segregation laws separated them from white people. Black people had to use separate services and facilities. These services and facilities were often worse than those provided to white people. Civil rights activists wanted discrimination and segregation to end.

In addition to being a famous musician, Franklin was also a civil rights activist. She spoke out against racial discrimination. Her song "Respect" became an anthem of the civil rights movement. For these reasons, Obama chose her to sing at his inauguration.

## A HISTORIC PERFORMANCE

This was not the first time Franklin had performed at an inauguration ceremony. She had sung at the inaugurations of Presidents Jimmy Carter and Bill Clinton. But neither day compared to this one for her. She was not nervous. She was excited to be part of this historic event. She could not sleep for days after receiving the invitation.

The day of Obama's inauguration was cold. It was just 19 degrees Fahrenheit (−7°C). Franklin stood on the steps of the US Capitol Building. She wore a heavy coat,

**Franklin gave a concert at the Lincoln Memorial in Washington, DC, before President Bill Clinton's 1993 inauguration.**

a hat, and gloves. She sang "My Country 'Tis of Thee" into a microphone. The crowd went wild with applause.

But Franklin was not pleased with her performance. She did not like the way the cold air affected her voice. She insisted on heading straight to a recording studio afterward. She wanted to make a better version of the song for history. It was important to her that it sounded just right.

## BROUGHT TO TEARS

Franklin had been singing in front of audiences since she was a child. She received many awards during her long career. One of the biggest awards was the Presidential Medal of Freedom. President George W. Bush gave her this medal in 2005. The Presidential Medal of Freedom is the highest honor given to a US civilian, or a person who is not a member of the

## PERSPECTIVES
### BARACK OBAMA

In 2015 Franklin attended the Kennedy Center Honors in Washington, DC. This event recognizes performers and musicians. Franklin was there to help honor singer Carole King. King had cowritten one of Franklin's songs, "(You Make Me Feel Like) A Natural Woman." Franklin performed the song. Barack Obama was in the audience. Obama later wrote, "Nobody embodies more fully the connection between the African-American spiritual, the blues, R. & B., rock and roll—the way that hardship and sorrow were transformed into something full of beauty and vitality and hope. American history wells up when Aretha sings."

US military. It is awarded to people who make important contributions to the country. Bush chose Franklin because her music had changed the nation. Her songs had become part of the country's cultural heritage.

Franklin was a deeply admired musician and activist. Her songs were a driving force for African Americans in their fight for equal rights. Franklin also broke down barriers for women. Her career was a shining example of the change that is possible when people are willing to stand up and demand to be treated with respect.

## EXPLORE ONLINE

Chapter One discusses the role Franklin and her music played in the civil rights movement. The article at the website below explores how music inspired civil rights activists. Does the article answer any of the questions you had about the civil rights movement?

VOICES OF STRUGGLE
abdocorelibrary.com/aretha-franklin

Franklin was moved when she received the Presidential Medal of Freedom in 2005. She clasped her hands together and cried.

# EARLY YEARS

Aretha Franklin was born on March 25, 1942, in Memphis, Tennessee. But she spent most of her childhood in Michigan after her family moved to Detroit. They were part of the Great Migration. This movement brought more than 6 million African Americans from the southern states to other parts of the country between 1916 and 1970. They were seeking more opportunities. They hoped to find better jobs. They also wanted to escape racial violence. State and local laws enforced segregation in the South. White hate groups such as the Ku Klux Klan were powerful there. They attacked and even killed many African Americans. Black migrants hoped they would find less

Aretha, *right*, poses with her father, C. L. Franklin, *middle*, and her sister Carolyn Franklin, *left*, in 1971.

15

# AFRICAN AMERICANS IN DETROIT

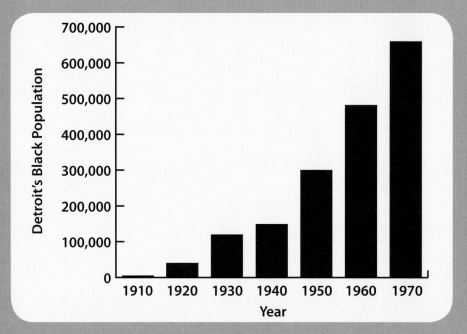

This graph shows the population of African Americans in Detroit from 1910 to 1970. This was the period of the Great Migration. How did the population change in these years? What trends do you notice?

discrimination and violence in the North. But life was still hard for many African Americans throughout the country.

Music was part of Aretha's childhood. Her mother, Barbara Siggers Franklin, played the piano. She was also a gospel singer. Gospel is type of religious music.

Aretha's father, Clarence LaVaughn Franklin, was a well-known minister. Many people called him C. L. He preached at the New Bethel Baptist Church in Detroit. He recorded some of his sermons with the record company Chess Records. The sermons were the speeches he gave when he preached at church. C. L. was also a singer.

Aretha's parents separated when she was just six years old. She and her siblings lived in Detroit with their father after the breakup. They spent the summers with their mother in Buffalo, New York.

When Aretha was nine years old, her mother died from a heart attack. C. L. then raised Aretha and her siblings on his own.

## EARLY CAREER

Like her mother's music, C. L.'s sermons made a strong impression on Aretha. C. L. traveled across the country to give sermons. Aretha often went with him. She sang gospel songs in front of large audiences at these events.

New Bethel Baptist Church, the church where C. L. preached, still stands in Detroit today.

People quickly noticed that this young girl had some major talent.

Aretha recorded her first album at the age of 14. It was called *Songs of Faith*. On the album, Aretha sang and also played the piano. Most of the music was recorded as she performed at her father's church in Detroit. Many of her earliest fans thought she was destined to become a professional gospel singer.

## CHALLENGES

Despite her budding music career, Aretha did not have an easy adolescence. Just a few years after losing her mother, a teenage Aretha became a mother herself. Her son Clarence was born in 1955. She gave birth to another son named Edward in 1957. Aretha was 14 years old at the time. Many people judged teen

**PERSPECTIVES**
RACISM IN THE SOUTH

Aretha and her father experienced racism as they toured the country, especially in the South. Many restaurants, hotels, and other establishments would not serve them. These places had signs that read "Whites Only." Many gas stations would not even allow Black people to use their restrooms. But Aretha and her father did not let this discrimination discourage them. They both believed change was possible.

mothers harshly. They disapproved of unmarried women having children. But C. L. did not scold or shame his daughter. He helped her as much as he could. He managed her singing career.

## TOURING

When she was 16 years old, Aretha seized a new opportunity. Her father was a civil rights activist. He was friends with civil rights leader Martin Luther King Jr. King traveled throughout the country to raise awareness of civil rights issues. One important issue was voting rights. In the South, lawmakers had created obstacles that kept Black people from voting. Black people had to pay a

### A MUSICAL GENIUS

Aretha dropped out of high school to focus on her music career and take care of her children. Aretha was very smart. She taught herself how to play the piano. She learned without even knowing how to read music. Two renowned schools gave her honorary degrees later in life. Berklee College of Music and Yale University honored her with doctoral degrees in music.

fine or pass a difficult test before they could register to vote. King was planning a voting rights campaign. He would travel across the country and help Black people register to vote. Aretha asked her father if she could tour with King. Her father agreed. She supported King and traveled with him on his campaign. King and other activists would later inspire her music.

## FURTHER EVIDENCE

Chapter Two discusses Aretha's childhood and early career. What was one of the main points of this chapter? What evidence is included to support this point? The video at the website below goes into more depth on Aretha's early years. Does the information on the website support the main point of the chapter? Does it present new evidence?

REMEMBERING ARETHA FRANKLIN
abdocorelibrary.com/aretha-franklin

# GAINING RESPECT

Aretha loved gospel music. But she wanted to perform other types of music as well. Like many other teenagers, she was drawn to Black pop music. She dreamed of singing rhythm and blues (R&B) songs. R&B combines many different styles of music. These styles include the blues, soul music, and pop music. Soul music evolved from gospel music. African Americans created this style of music. It features strong vocals.

Some R&B and other nonreligious music had sexual messages. Because of this, many religious parents did not approve of

Aretha sings at a recording session in Columbia Studios in 1962.

nonreligious music. Some parents only allowed their children to listen to gospel songs. But Aretha's father did not mind that Aretha was interested in different types of music. He appreciated each artist's unique style. He believed talent should always be encouraged. He was friends with many Black singers and musicians. He welcomed them into his home. Visitors sang while Aretha accompanied them on the piano.

Dinah Washington, Sam Cooke, and Mahalia Jackson were among the famous singers who visited the Franklins' home. Aretha looked to them as examples of Black singers who had successful careers. All three of them sang gospel music. Washington and Cooke later crossed over into other styles of music, including pop music. Soon Aretha would do the same.

## CHANGES

In 1960 Aretha decided to record a pop album. She was 18 years old at the time. Her father stayed on as her manager. He helped her find a record label. C. L. was

Singer Mahalia Jackson inspired Aretha from an early age.

friends with record producer Berry Gordy. Gordy owned Motown Records in Detroit. He tried to sign Aretha to his record label. Motown Records later became popular. But at the time, it was still a new label. Aretha decided to sign with Columbia Records instead. This record label was well known worldwide. Aretha and her father thought this label could better promote her music.

Columbia Records was in New York City. Aretha had to move there from Detroit. She felt good about this career decision. But she knew it was going to require a lot of hard work. It also meant leaving behind her children in Detroit. Her grandmother and sister cared for them while she was away.

Shortly after her move, Aretha met a man named Ted White. They married one year later in 1961. Ted became Aretha's new manager.

In 1963 C. L. helped Mahalia Jackson organize a civil rights rally in Chicago. This event took place on May 27. Aretha performed at the rally along with several other entertainers.

## SWITCHING LABELS

In 1964 Franklin and White had a child together. They named him Ted White Jr. He inherited his mother's love of music. When he grew up, he played backup guitar in her band.

**Franklin married Ted White when she was 19 years old.**

Franklin made ten albums with Columbia Records. Critics praised her music. Still, the albums she made with the label did not sell as well as other pop artists' albums. Columbia Records did not take advantage of Franklin's powerful voice and musical style. They asked her to record many cover songs, or songs that other famous singers had already released. Franklin wanted more control over her musical arrangements. She also wanted to record songs that she had written herself.

When the time came to re-sign with Columbia Records, Franklin considered other labels. Atlantic Records made her an offer that suited her better. This label wanted her to write and record original music. Atlantic Records would also allow her to use her sisters as backup singers. Franklin made the move to Atlantic Records in 1966.

## CREATING AN ANTHEM

Atlantic Records kept its promise to give Franklin more creative control. One of her first songs with the label was a cover of Otis Redding's song "Respect." Franklin sang it in a way that made the song her own. In the original song, Redding asks a woman to treat him with respect. Franklin's version switches the gender roles. Franklin explains all of the sacrifices a woman has to make for a man. She asks to be treated with respect.

Civil rights activists soon adopted "Respect" as an anthem. An anthem is a song that has special importance for a group of people. It represents the group's causes and ideals. Civil rights activists asked for African Americans to be treated with respect. In this way, they identified with the song. It became an anthem for the women's rights movement too. Women's rights activists wanted women to be treated equally. "Respect" asks for women to be treated with the same respect as men.

## FRANKLIN'S MUSIC

Franklin's songs were often upbeat. They made people want to get up and dance. Her music also expressed important messages. Martin Luther King Jr.'s daughter Bernice King respected Aretha as both a musician and an activist. Bernice said, "As a daughter of the [civil rights] movement, she [Aretha] not only used her voice to entertain but to uplift and inspire generations through songs that have become anthems."

People within the music industry also recognized the cultural importance of "Respect." Franklin won two Grammy Awards for the song in 1968. One was for best R&B recording. Another was for best R&B solo vocal performance by a woman.

Franklin followed up "Respect" with another big hit. She cowrote "Think" with her husband. This was their last success together. Franklin's marriage to White was not a happy one. Franklin's friends reported that he was abusive toward her. The couple divorced in 1969.

# STRAIGHT TO THE
# SOURCE

In a 2018 article for *Rolling Stone* magazine, music journalist Mikal Gilmore described Franklin's influence. He wrote:

> *Franklin's voice raised and defined her. Nobody came close to touching it, though she emboldened many others to follow her—Patti LaBelle, Gladys Knight, Natalie Cole, Chaka Khan, Whitney Houston, Alicia Keys and Beyoncé among them. More than any of them, Franklin possessed a roar that wasn't merely technically breathtaking; it was also a natural . . . instrument that testified to her truths in ways she otherwise refused to address. Some say Franklin was insecure at times in her gift, but with something so fearsome moving through their body, mind and history, who wouldn't be both daunted and proud?*

> Source: Mikal Gilmore. "The Queen." *Rolling Stone*. Rolling Stone, September 27, 2018. Web. Accessed May 30, 2019.

## Consider Your Audience

Adapt this passage for a different audience, such as your friends. Write a blog post conveying this same information for the new audience. How does your post differ from the original text and why?

# CHAPTER
# FOUR

# LATER LIFE AND LEGACY

F ranklin's career took off in the 1960s. She had many hit songs. Her songs appeared on both the R&B and pop music charts.

In the midst of her success, Franklin experienced a tragedy. On April 4, 1968, Martin Luther King Jr. was assassinated. It was a personal loss for Franklin. But she also felt the loss as people across the nation did. One of the greatest civil rights leaders was now gone. Franklin sang at King's funeral on April 9 in Memphis.

Franklin's performance at King's funeral gained her even more recognition.

**Franklin poses with some of her hit records in the late 1960s.**

In June 1968, she appeared on the cover of *Time* magazine. An article in the magazine called her Lady Soul. Soon her nickname would change to the Queen of Soul.

The 1970s began with happier life events for Franklin. She was now in a relationship with her road manager, Ken Cunningham. In 1970 they welcomed a son. They named him Kecalf.

Franklin's relationship with Cunningham did not last. In 1977 she met actor Glynn Turman. She married him one year later at her father's church in Detroit. C. L. performed the wedding ceremony.

Another tragedy struck Franklin and her family in June 1979. Franklin had just finished performing in Las Vegas, Nevada, when she received horrible news. Her father had been shot during a robbery in his home in Detroit. By the time she arrived at the hospital, her father had slipped into a coma. He never woke up. He died five years later. He had instilled strong religious

**Franklin poses with her husband Glynn Turman, *left*, and son Kecalf in the late 1970s.**

beliefs in his children. Franklin credited her faith for helping her through the loss of her father.

## MAKING A COMEBACK

In 1980 Franklin made an appearance on the big screen. She played a waitress in the hit comedy *The Blues Brothers*. Franklin performed her song "Think" in the movie. This helped introduce the song to a new generation of fans.

Franklin decided to change record labels again in that same year. This time she signed with Arista Records. Then in 1985 she released an album called *Who's Zoomin' Who?* It produced three hit singles. "Freeway of Love" rose to the number one spot on *Billboard*'s Hot R&B chart. Another hit single was a duet with singer Annie Lennox. It was called "Sisters Are Doin' It for Themselves." This song reminded many fans of the feminist values Franklin had expressed in "Respect." Franklin's third hit single from the album was another duet. She recorded the song "I Knew You Were Waiting (For Me)" with singer George Michael.

In 1987 Franklin received an important honor. She was inducted into the Rock & Roll Hall of Fame. She was the first woman to receive this honor.

Over the next two decades, Franklin continued to record albums. She also added many Grammy Awards

In 1998, a sequel to *The Blues Brothers* was released. Franklin appeared in the sequel.

to her list of accomplishments. She won 18 Grammys throughout her career.

## A MUSICAL LEGEND

Franklin rarely spoke about her private life. She was diagnosed with pancreatic cancer in her later years.

She did not share this diagnosis with fans. In 2010 one of Franklin's relatives shared the news.

Few people live with pancreatic cancer as long as Franklin did. Even after her diagnosis, she continued to perform. She also released a few albums. Her last public performance happened in New York City in November 2017. She died on August 16, 2018, in Detroit. She was 76 years old.

Tributes soon flooded social media. Franklin's fans expressed their gratitude for her music. Many people in the music industry shared how Franklin had influenced them.

## STEPPING UP

In 1998 opera singer Luciano Pavarotti was scheduled to perform at the Grammy Awards. However, he fell ill shortly before the ceremony. Franklin agreed to take his place. Opera was one musical genre Franklin was not known for. She also did not have any time to rehearse. Still, she performed the opera song "Nessun Dorma." The crowd cheered and clapped after she had finished. Many people praised her performance.

# FRANKLIN'S HITS

| SONG | YEAR RELEASED |
|---|---|
| (You Make Me Feel Like) A Natural Woman | 1967 |
| Chain of Fools | 1968 |
| I Say a Little Prayer | 1968 |
| Think | 1968 |
| Freeway of Love | 1985 |
| Sisters Are Doin' It for Themselves | 1985 |
| Who's Zoomin' Who | 1985 |

This chart shows some of Franklin's biggest hits and the years in which they were released. Does this chart help you better understand Franklin's career and influence? Why or why not?

Franklin's funeral was held on August 31, 2018. It lasted more than six hours. The event was live-streamed. It included performances and speeches. Bill Clinton and civil rights leader Jesse Jackson attended the funeral. So did many entertainers, including Jennifer Hudson, Ariana Grande, and Stevie Wonder.

Franklin's songs encouraged people to fight for what they believed in. Decades after the civil rights movement, this is still the case. African Americans fight racial injustice and police brutality through the Black Lives Matter movement. Women are using the hashtag #MeToo to share their stories of sexual abuse and harassment. This can make people feel empowered to fight abuse and harassment. Franklin's words and her music inspire these people. Her spirit will live on through her music for generations to come.

# STRAIGHT TO THE
# SOURCE

In a 2018 interview, Detroit artist and producer John Sims reflected on Franklin's influence and the importance of her music. He said:

*Her love and advocacy for black people was undeniable and her feminism unshakable. Before there [was] Black Lives Matter and #MeToo, the Queen was challenging us to "think" and "respect" ourselves. . . .*

*She became extremely blessed and successful, [but] she never forgot her roots, her people. . . . We owe Ms. Aretha Franklin our highest respect for being the voice of our most meaningful form of human intelligence: love. To honor her is to follow her many messages and examples of love, grace and community.*

Source: David A. Love. "How Aretha Franklin's Commitment to Civil Rights and Equality Changed Hearts and Minds." *NBC News*. NBC News, August 16, 2018. Web. Accessed May 30, 2019.

## What's the Big Idea?
Take a close look at this passage. What connections did Sims make between Franklin and the civil rights and women's rights movements? How does he trace Franklin's influence to modern movements?

# FAST FACTS

- Aretha Franklin was born in Memphis, Tennessee, on March 25, 1942.

- Franklin's mother played piano and sang gospel music. Franklin's father was a well-known minister and civil rights activist. He was also a singer.

- When Franklin was nine years old, her mother died from a heart attack.

- Franklin toured the country with her father as he delivered sermons. She sang gospel music at these events.

- At the age of 14, Franklin recorded her first album. It was called *Songs of Faith*.

- Franklin and her father were involved in the civil rights movement. Martin Luther King Jr. was a friend of the Franklin family.

- At the age of 18, Franklin signed with Columbia Records and moved to New York City.

- In 1967 Franklin released her hit song "Respect." The song reached number one on the *Billboard* pop music chart. It also became an anthem of the civil rights and women's rights movements.

- In 1987 Franklin became the first woman to be inducted into the Rock & Roll Hall of Fame.

- Franklin sang at Barack Obama's presidential inauguration in 2009.

- Franklin died on August 16, 2018, at the age of 76.

# STOP AND
# THINK

### Surprise Me

This book discusses Aretha Franklin's work as both a singer
and a civil rights activist. After reading this book, what
two or three facts about Franklin's life did you find most
surprising? Write a few sentences about each fact. Why did
you find each fact surprising?

### You Are There

This book describes Franklin's performance at Barack
Obama's 2009 inauguration ceremony. Imagine that you
attended this historic event. Write a letter to a friend or
family member about the experience. Be sure to add plenty
of details to your letter.

### Why Do I Care?

Franklin took part in the American civil rights movement.
This movement happened more than 50 years ago. How is
the civil rights movement's influence still visible today? How
do you think the movement affects your life or the lives of
others? What might your classroom or community be like if
this movement had not taken place?

# GLOSSARY

**arrangement**
the way a song is performed by a particular artist

**assassinate**
to kill someone for political reasons

**discrimination**
the unjust treatment of a group of people based on their race, gender, or other characteristics

**feminist**
a person who believes in equal rights regardless of sex or gender

**genre**
a category of music

**inauguration**
a ceremony that celebrates a new president taking office

**induct**
to make someone a member of a group or organization

**racism**
the belief that one race is better than others

**R&B**
short for "rhythm and blues," R&B is a style of music that combines blues, pop, and other types of music

**segregation**
the separation of people into groups based on race or other factors

# ONLINE
# RESOURCES

To learn more about Aretha Franklin, visit our free resource websites below.

Visit **abdocorelibrary.com** or scan this QR code for free Common Core resources for teachers and students, including vetted activities, multimedia, and booklinks, for deeper subject comprehension.

Visit **abdobooklinks.com** or scan this QR code for free additional online weblinks for further learning. These links are routinely monitored and updated to provide the most current information available.

# LEARN
# MORE

Baxter, Roberta. *Women in Music*. Minneapolis, MN: Abdo Publishing, 2019.

Terp, Gail. *Nonviolent Resistance in the Civil Rights Movement*. Minneapolis, MN: Abdo Publishing, 2016.

# ABOUT THE
# AUTHORS

### Duchess Harris, JD, PhD

Dr. Harris is a professor of American Studies at Macalester College and curator of the Duchess Harris Collection of ABDO books. She is also the coauthor of the titles in the collection, which features popular selections such as *Hidden Human Computers: The Black Women of NASA* and series including News Literacy and Being Female in America.

Before working with ABDO, Dr. Harris authored several other books on the topics of race, culture, and American history. She served as an associate editor for *Litigation News*, the American Bar Association Section of Litigation's quarterly flagship publication, and was the first editor in chief of *Law Raza*, an interactive online journal covering race and the law, published at William Mitchell College of Law. She has earned a PhD in American Studies from the University of Minnesota and a JD from William Mitchell College of Law.

### Tammy Gagne

Tammy Gagne has written dozens of books for both adults and children. Her recent titles include *Carol Moseley Braun* and *Richard Wright*. She lives in northern New England with her husband, son, and a menagerie of pets.

# INDEX